INSIDE OUT FAITH

Study of the Book of James

SALLY BAKER

Cover Art & layout design by Juli Camarin.

This book is dedicated to my husband Ed...
A man who continues to humbly live out his heart faith
in the ever changing circumstances of our lives

CONTENTS

WHY THE BOOK OF JAMES?

For most of my life as a Christian, James has been a book of the New Testament that has both encouraged my faith and challenged me to venture deeper into my relationship with Jesus.

In many ways, this epistle seems to me like a bridge between the message and promises of the Old Testament and what Jesus taught about how a personal relationship with him can transform one's life.

James' own spiritual journey was not without very familiar bumps in the road and potholes until he came to the place where he recognized Jesus as the Messiah and his savior.

Suddenly the direction that his life was headed totally changed, and he became a follower of the one who is the Way, the Truth, and the Life.

James' writing is both passionate and practical and has much wisdom to share with us about living our faith from the inside out.

JUST JAMES... A MESSAGE FROM THE HEART

James' letter was one of the first New Testament books to be written (ca 50-60 AD) and is unique in several respects. Both the characteristics of his writing and the content of what he wrote reflect his own spiritual journey. He begins (James 1:1) by identifying himself in a very humble way as the servant—or slave—of God and Jesus the Messiah. His attitude is no longer that of the skeptical brother who had openly dared Jesus to prove himself. James has now embraced both the fullness of who Jesus was and the importance of the message he taught. Knowing Jesus as the Messiah and sharing that truth with others has become his life.

James had lived all of his life as an observant Jew for whom the content of the Old Testament—the Law and the Prophets—was extremely important. For many Jews, this emphasis on what the law said and keeping all its requirements, plus many other rules that had been added by the Pharisees, was what determined their righteousness. In observant Jewish communities like Nazareth, that mindset would have been the accepted norm. Ritual and legalism were seen as being a good thing and a way of earning God's approval and the respect of one's fellow Jews.

However, in his ministry as the leader of the fellowship of Christians in Jerusalem and from his own experience, James knew that empty legalism—religion worn on the outside—was not what a relationship with God was about. Jesus had made it absolutely clear how real faith is based on knowing God in a personal way. (John 3:16) Real faith radiates from the inside out. James wanted his fellow Jews to whom he was writing, to understand how Jesus has brought the completion and fulfillment of what the Old Testament had said. (Matt. 5:17)

Because of his own background and the fact that he was writing to Christian Jews of the Diaspora, James' letter has a very Jewish style in what it says and the language he uses. For example, he refers to the body of believers using the Greek word for *'synagogue'* rather than the word for *'church'*. (James 2:2) There are similarities between James' letter and the Old Testament book of Proverbs in the way he gives practical and wise counsel for dealing with the daily realities of one's life as a follower of Jesus. As Jesus frequently did in his teaching, James used word pictures and parables, both of which are common in Hebrew literature. James also wrote as someone very well versed in the Jewish Torah, and therefore, his style of writing would have sounded very familiar to his Jewish audience.

Because as an observant Jew, James knew very well what it was to look at one's spiritual life from the outside in, he was passionate about sharing what it meant to be born again and have the heart transformed on the inside.

Jesus had used light as a powerful picture in his own teaching (Matt. 5:14-16) when he taught (The Sermon on the Mount) on a hillside on the northern shore of the Sea of Galilee. Built on a hill directly across the lake near the eastern shore was a city called Hippos. At night the lights of that city would have been clearly visible from far away across the lake.

The truth that James had personally come to know was that like Hippos—a city whose light James would often have seen—our light should glow with a warmth and brilliance that would draw others to a transforming relationship with Jesus. James understood this principle well. All his life as a part of Jesus' immediate family and an observer of his ministry as a rabbi, he had been connected to Jesus from the outside, and yet he had deliberately closed his heart to what Jesus taught and its implications for his own life. That is, until he was confronted with the undeniable truth of who Jesus was and came to know him as the Son of God and the Light of the World. From that point on, it was the inside relationship with God that fueled the lamp of James' faith, and being a light-bearer became his calling for the remainder of his life.

As we consider these fundamental principles of belief and life—concepts just as relevant today as they were 2000 years ago—we will first pull back the curtain of time and examine the spiritual journeys of both James and Paul to discover why this topic was so important in both of their personal lives and ministries. We will also take a careful look at scriptures that address the dynamic relationship of knowing what it means to be a Christian and actually entering into a relationship with God through the salvation Jesus offers, and how being 'born again' in that way transforms one's life. Then we will carefully examine the letter James wrote to those first Jewish Christians and consider how his words connect and apply to our own faith journeys today. Although we will primarily focus on the very practical words of wisdom on how to live 'Christianly' that we find in the letter James wrote to the first Jewish Christians, we will also look at how his letter echoes the teaching of Jesus and is in harmony with the content of the letters of Paul.

A WORD ABOUT FAITH & WORKS

What matters most—genuine faith or good works? The question is as old as mankind's relationship with God; and since the beginning of time the debate about the answer to that question has continued. Is true religion a matter of the heart, or is it determined by the way we act?

Over and over again throughout the history of Israel, the pendulum of popular opinion about how faith and works are related seemed to swing first one way, then the other. However, the resounding message that consistently rings out from the pages of scripture, whether proclaimed by the words of the prophets or played out in the actual events of Israel's history, is that both are absolutely essential for a solid and real relationship with God to exist on both a personal and a national level.

Very simply, the two components—faith and works—cannot be separated or biblical truth is twisted, spiritual realities are wrongly defined, and a false standard of superficial 'religiosity' becomes the accepted norm—usually with profoundly negative results.

The biblical principal is very clear: one's relationship with God begins in the heart. There must be a life-altering realization that sin is real, that its consequences are fatal, and that faith in who God is and the redemption He has promised is the only solution. When we accept the Covenant relationship God has offered and allow His atoning love to transform us from the inside out, that new spiritual reality will be demonstrated by the way we live. Others will know what we believe by what we do and what we say.

On one hand, it sounds so simple—inside and outside—all part of the same whole; and yet the fact is that for thousands of years various distortions of that simple truth have led to heretical teaching, hypocritical attitudes, and hardened hearts. All throughout his ministry Jesus confronted these foundational issues of faith and life. And over and over again he cut to the heart of the matter: the salvation he personified had the power to make life new—to light the flame of faith that would transform the believer into one who would become a light to the world. (Matt. 5:14)

As we might expect, the relationship of faith and works—spirituality from the outside in or the inside out—was something that was of great importance to the leaders of the early church. Both in Jewish and in Gentile contexts, although they may have come from differing cultural perspectives, a clear understanding of the right relationship of faith and works was critical for the Body of Christ to flourish and grow.

The situation we face today is amazingly, very much the same. Faith and works are still hot-button issues. The concepts of inside out or outside in are as relevant for us as they were for the first Jewish Christians in Jerusalem ministered to by James and for the Gentile believers evangelized and discipled by Paul on his mission trips.

For both James and Paul coming to understand personally who Jesus was and accepting the salvation he offered had completely transformed their lives, and sharing that powerful truth of the gospel they had personally experienced became their passion. What they wrote about the outside in and inside out of their own faith journeys can speak deeply to the circumstances of our own lives.

Because this balance of faith and works is so important and foundational to what it means to be a Christian, it is perhaps no surprise that these principles were some of the first aspects of doctrine bent and twisted into dangerous heresies that had the potential for perverting the truth of the gospel message and its power to transform lives.

The first of these heresies has been labeled the Judiazing heresy. It was embraced primarily by Jews who held tightly to the belief that faith in the atonement Jesus had provided when he died on the cross and the redemption his death and resurrection had accomplished had to be accompanied by a strict adherence to Old Testament law. This perspective on faith and works very commonly morphed into a very strict and legalistic kind of pietism. Those who promoted this extremely legalistic view insisted that Gentile believers could not really become Christians unless they first became Jewish proselytes and followed all the Jewish laws and traditions. The inherent danger in this heretical view was minimizing or negating the importance of the truth that there is nothing we can do—no way we can earn credits or points—no list of good works we can accumulate—that can make us righteous, remove our sin, or accomplish our salvation.

"For it is by grace you have been saved through faith… not by works." (Eph. 2:8-9)

On the other extreme, there developed a second heresy called *antinomianism.* This twisting of truth has a long name, but a fairly simple premise: As long as a person said he believed the gospel, that settled the matter. Practically speaking, their view regarded however that person lived, whatever words he spoke, how he treated others, or whatever he did with his physical body as basically irrelevant. Head knowledge and mere verbal assent were all that mattered. Obviously this attitude, although its leniency was appealing in some respects, was extremely spiritually unhealthy to individuals who embraced its 'anything goes' mentality and could cause great damage to a fellowship of believers and the perception others had of what it meant to be a Christian.

Unfortunately, these two heretical ways of thinking are still very much alive and well today. They may have had a variety of different names attached to them since the first century, but they have not gone away and continue to have the potential for doing as much damage in the present as they did in the early years of the church. Salvation cannot be earned by self-righteously following a legalistic code of behavior, nor is it merely a concept we give a nod to in a politically correct way but has no impact on how we live.

Both for James, as he led the Jerusalem fellowship which was primarily made up of Jewish believers in Jesus, and for Paul, as he evangelized and discipled Gentile Christians across the Roman world, having a clear understanding of how faith and good works intersected in one's life as a Christian was extremely important. What was it that really mattered - inside out or outside in?

JAMES AND PAUL...
TWO MEN TRANSFORMED
FROM THE INSIDE OUT

What would it have been like to grow up with Jesus as your older brother? Although the gospels don't tell us much about that family aspect of Jesus' life, there are several very reasonable conclusions we can draw that do give us some perspective on the circumstances and events that shaped James' personality and faith.

Both Mary and Joseph were descended from the family line of David with close enough extended immediate family connections in Bethlehem that they were required to travel there to register for the Roman census at the time of Jesus' birth. Why would families like theirs with such direct ties to Bethlehem have moved over 60 miles north and settled in a small out-of-the-way town like Nazareth? Perhaps the answer at least partially lies in the occupation of Joseph's family—something that in their culture was commonly passed on from one generation to another.

Bethlehem is only a few miles south of Jerusalem; between those two cities stood the Herodian, a magnificent and well-fortified compound that had been designed to be both a pleasure palace and strategic military stronghold. Herod the Great had constructed the Herodian to serve as a luxurious retreat to entertain guests and a well-defended place of safety not far from Jerusalem if he happened to be threatened with any kind of political unrest.

Because the members of Joseph's family were probably builders by trade and because of the Herodian's close proximity to Bethlehem, they would undoubtedly have been conscripted as laborers for its construction. Such a decisive move away from Bethlehem to Nazareth may have been a result of their very deliberate refusal to be forced into serving a king who was both feared for his iron-fisted rule and regarded with distain because of his corrupt moral values and his well known manipulation of Temple Judaism to accomplish his own agenda and control.

Nazareth was a very small community of less than 500 people, far away from the power struggles and politics of Judea—a tiny rural village where observant Jews could live out their faith without fear of any interference that might come from such a corrupt political system. It was a town in the middle of nowhere with no historical claim to fame. It was so unimportant ,it is not mentioned in the Old Testament or in the writings of Josephus or the Talmud's listing of towns in the Galilee. It was essentially 'no place'. In fact, at one point before meeting Jesus, the disciple Nathaniel made the rather sarcastic comment that "indeed nothing good could come from Nazareth." (John 1:46)

However, even though it was so small—about 60 acres—and off the beaten path, it had an active synagogue which undoubtedly would also have been an important part of the daily life of Jesus and his family. Not only would it have been the center of their community and their place of worship, but, as the custom was at that time, it would have been the school Jesus and his brothers attended where they learned basic skills like reading and writing and were thoroughly immersed in the content and importance of the scriptures.

We know from the accounts in Luke's gospel of Mary and Joseph taking Jesus to the Temple as an infant and again when he was around 12 or 13, probably for his Bar Mitzvah, that observing the requirements of the Law and religious traditions were important to them. It seems a reasonable assumption to conclude that those traditions and the respect of scripture they demonstrated were a continuing part of their family's life, and that James would have grown up experiencing how those acts of faithful obedience defined both how one worshipped and one's relationship to God.

Since it was the usual way families operated, Jesus and his brothers would have learned Joseph's trade as a builder and participated in carrying on the family business. The term 'carpenter' that is used implies the use of more construction skills than woodworking, though that would certainly have been an important part of their work.

Nazareth was only 4 miles from a city rebuilt by Herod Antipas who had inherited the territory of the Galilee from Herod the Great. This elaborate rebuilding of Sephhoris into the most opulent city in the region took place during the lifetime of Joseph and his sons. Consequently, it is very possible they would have worked on some of the construction projects there.

We know that Jesus was about 30 when he began his ministry as an itinerant teaching rabbi. Since Joseph is not mentioned at that point in the gospels, it is reasonable to assume he had died prior to that time. As the oldest son, Jesus would therefore have been the head of the family, and leaving his profession as a carpenter to begin his ministry would have passed that responsibility of familial leadership on to James. (Because James is always listed first when Jesus' brothers are named, he might very well have been older than his brothers Joseph, Simon, and Jude.)

In John 2, at the very beginning of Jesus' ministry shortly after his baptism by John the Baptist, Jesus and some of his disciples attended a wedding celebration in Cana, another small village near Nazareth. (Jn. 2:1-11) The fact that Jesus and his disciples were all invited to the feast and Mary was concerned about the supply of wine being gone are indications that the wedding could have been that of one of his sisters or another close relative.

As John noted, this was the first of Jesus' miracles and opened the eyes of those who witnessed it to see him in a whole new light. Following the wedding, Jesus went to Capernaum—the town on the northwest shore of the Sea of Galilee that would become the base of operations for his ministry. He was accompanied by Mary, his brothers, and his disciples and they all remained there for a few days. It would seem at this point that Jesus had the willing support of his brothers. But that was about to change.

Luke's gospel records the events of a Sabbath when Jesus returned to Nazareth and was given the opportunity to be the guest teacher, something that he also frequently did in other towns. (Lk. 4:14-30) By this time people in Nazareth had certainly heard of what Jesus had been teaching and the miracles he had performed; there seemed to be almost a sense of excitement and pride in claiming Jesus as a 'hometown boy' who was making a name for himself as a well-known rabbi. They knew his family, were familiar with their construction business, and were very impressed by the way Jesus spoke. That is... until he got to the heart of the issue. After reading Isaiah 61:1-2, Jesus made a very clear statement of who he was and his mission as the Messiah promised by the prophets. Although Nazareth was willing to see him as a popular rabbi, they were not ready to accept him as the savior who had the power to transform lives. Then Jesus went further to make it clear that their lack of faith would prevent them from experiencing the miracles and the kind of teaching other communities had experienced. At that point the mood changed. They no longer saw his Nazareth roots as a positive thing; but rather, taking offense at his words, turned the fact of his humble beginnings around. Who did he—a carpenter from Nazareth—think that he was! He could no longer be admired as one of their own. They were unable to process what he had said about Gentiles being more open to the gospel than they were, and their anger suddenly became violent. The hometown crowd turned into a mob and tried to throw him over the high cliff on which Nazareth was built.

What kind of effect did this incident have on Jesus' family? It is safe to assume that it must have impacted them in many ways and was probably both troubling and frightening. In Matthew 12:48-50, we see them attempting what looks like an 'intervention' or a desperate attempt to get Jesus out of the public eye and talk some sense to him. Jesus, however, drew a line: He redefined his 'family' as those who heard his teaching as the Word of God and embraced it. Jesus' reply was not a rejection of his family, but an affirmation of the importance of his spiritual relationship with those who believed in him.

From this point on, the gospels are silent about Jesus' brothers until fairly late in his ministry (Jn 7:1-5), just prior to the fall feast of Tabernacles when many Jews went to Jerusalem to worship. They were strongly urging Jesus to go to Jerusalem—something he had often done before—not just to celebrate these holy days, but so that he could use this opportunity to make his ministry more public. John made clear that their words were not meant as encouragement, but were rather a result of their own lack of belief in what he taught. They were taunting him to prove himself in a very public way. Jesus did go to the feast, but on his own terms and in his own timing. His teaching during that week about who he was and his mission was powerful, and his miraculous healing of a man born blind certainly got the attention of those who witnessed it and of the Temple authorities. However, what he said and did were not done merely to win popular acclaim as his brothers had challenged him to do.

The next time we read about James is after the resurrection. What happened during those intervening months is not recorded. How did James process the things he had heard Jesus say and the miracles he had witnessed with his own eyes? What were the frustrations and the anger that festered in his heart as he took the role of the head of the family in Nazareth? Did he resent the furor that Jesus' teaching in the synagogue had caused? How could he reconcile the very real faith of his upbringing, the respect he had for God's Word, and his ingrained value of keeping the law with what his older brother was doing and saying? How did he feel about his mother's deep conviction that Jesus was fulfilling some kind of divine destiny?

Probably all of his life, James had followed the godly values and principles he had learned from his parents who had very personally experienced the amazing and tangible reality of God's presence in their lives. Living life God's way as an observant Jew was undoubtedly just the way life was lived in his home and very familiar and important to him. But what about his heart? Had he personally embraced a faith relationship with God? Or was the righteous persona that defined him something that he wore like a religious garment? Did the words that his brother spoke and the way he pulled back tradition and revealed the truth behind it cause James to wrap that garment even more tightly and protectively around himself?

Even though we do not have a lot of details about Paul's early years, we are provided with enough information—mostly from the words of Paul himself—to get a good picture of what characterized him before his life-changing encounter with Jesus on the road to Damascus. Paul was from a Jewish family living in Tarsus in Cilicia which he described as "no ordinary city". (Acts 21:39) Not only was it an important commercial center with its own university, but it was also situated at a significant crossroads of travel on the Cyndus River. We also know that Paul was born into a family that had the status of being Roman citizens, which carried with it important rights and privileges. Although his family did not live within the geographic boundaries of Israel, their Jewish heritage was evidently of great importance to them and they were zealous concerning their faith as observant Jews. On more than one occasion Paul mentions that when he was old enough he went to live in Jerusalem so that he could study under Gamaliel who was the most honored rabbi of the first century and who is mentioned several times in the New Testament.

In Philippians 3:4-11 Paul described the level of self-righteous pride that had once defined him. He had worn this legalistic religious passion like a garment that he believed set him apart and above the ordinary. He felt such confidence in what he saw as the spiritual authority he felt he had earned as a Pharisee that he saw it as a 'mitzvah' or good work to single out and persecute those who had put their faith in Jesus. He was judgmental enough to willingly approve of Stephen's execution by stoning because of Stephen's powerful testimony as a Christian or Follower of the Way and aggressive enough to pursue believers in Jesus as Israel's Messiah all the way to Damascus with the intent of arresting them and returning them to Jerusalem as prisoners.

Paul the Pharisee was on fire with a religious zeal that primarily came from his strict legalistic observance of Jewish laws and traditions. To him, like many other Pharisees, keeping the letter of the law was the greatest good—striving for this legalistic perfection was what had come to define him and affirmed his prestige and reputation as a strict Pharisee.

Paul & James

Paul and James were two men from very different backgrounds, yet both were confronted with the question of who Jesus really was and how what he taught, the things he did, and the transforming impact of his message were to be reconciled with their own faith journeys.

Paul identified this pivotal turning point for both of them in 1 Corinthians 15 as he described the foundational importance of the resurrection. If the resurrection of Jesus did not occur, Paul asserted Christianity is the greatest of spiritual frauds. But if it did indeed happen, it is the undeniable proof positive of all that Jesus taught and the irrefutable evidence of who he is and the power he has to forgive our sins, reconcile us to God, and give us the promise of eternal life. For both Paul and James, the evidence that stopped them (quite literally) in their tracks was their own personal encounters with Jesus after his resurrection.

At the beginning of Acts (1:14), we find James is no longer the critical skeptic he once was, but rather a part of the core group of disciples and other believers in Jesus gathered in the upper room to pray and await the promised coming of the Holy Spirit. Later when James described himself at the beginning of his epistle, he called himself the servant of Jesus, his Lord and Messiah. His whole perspective on life had been radically changed.

After Paul's conversion on the road to Damascus (Acts 9), Paul returned to Jerusalem and spent some time with Peter and with James. (Acts 9:26-34; Gal. 1:11-24) Initially there undoubtedly must have been many questions about the sincerity of Paul's spiritual transformation because of his recent and well-known persecution of Christians. But they could see he was indeed a man made new—born again and now a part of the Body of Christ. Barnabas, another of the early Christians and leaders of the church, mentored Paul, served together with him in Antioch, and accompanied him on his first mission trip.

At the same time Paul's mission to take the Gospel to the Gentiles was continuing to grow, James was serving along with Peter and John and eventually became the leader of the Jewish Christians in Jerusalem. (Gal. 2:1-10) It was inevitable, given the cultural and religious tensions that existed, that there would be some serious issues involving how Jews and Gentiles could as Christians be on an equal footing as they stood in their relationship with God. The unity of the Body of Christ was of critical importance both to James and the other leaders of the Jewish believers and to Paul and those whose ministry was primarily to non-Jews. Led by the Holy Spirit, they met in Jerusalem to discuss those issues of faith and life— how rule-keeping and good works are related to a confession of belief. (Acts 15) For both James and Paul this council and its Spirit-led conclusions were of utmost importance. Real, sincere, transforming faith in the salvation Jesus accomplished on the cross is what is absolutely essential to becoming a Christian. And because it is real, that life-changing faith will be evident in every area of life—in the relationship we have with God, what we do, the words we say, the priorities we choose, and the interactions we have with others. (Gal. 3:26-29)

James and Paul were two men who had traveled on different roads, but they had carried the same baggage and had both arrived at the same destination because of having had a personal defining encounter with the resurrected Jesus along the way. Inside out and outside in—they had both discovered in a very personal way that if we separate the faith that saves us from the evidence of that faith's existence in our daily lives, an important piece of the new creation we have become is missing and the picture others see of that faith relationship will be faded and blurred.

THE IMPORTANCE OF FAITH…WHY 'STICKING IT OUT' MATTERS

The first chapter of James' epistle begins with an attention-getting statement: "Count it pure joy…whenever you face trials." (1:2) Given the world we live in today, being a believer in Jesus can frequently be a very difficult stand to take. During the first century when James wrote, when Jewish Christians publicly proclaimed their faith, it often meant being thrown out of a local synagogue and shunned by other Jews because of their belief in Jesus as the Messiah. Like Paul, James personally understood what it was to suffer for his faith in Jesus and for his out-spoken ministry of sharing the gospel with others. We can get a sense of how familiar James was with 'trials' from the Jewish historian Josephus, who was a contemporary of James and recorded some of what James experienced at the end of his life.

"Annus (the high priest)… thought he had now a proper opportunity to exercise his authority. Festus was now dead, and Albinus was but upon the road; so he assembled the Sanhedrin of judges, and brought before them the brother of Jesus, who was called Christ, whose name was James, and some others, (or some of his companions); and when he had formed an accusation against them as breakers of the law, he delivered them to be stoned; but as for those who seemed the most equitable of the citizens, and such as were the most uneasy at the breach of the laws, they disliked what was done…."

Josephus; The Antiquities of the Jews Book 20/9/1

For those Jewish believers to whom James initially wrote, it was a given that being a Christian was not going to be easy and Christian values then, as they are today, were often seen as counter-cultural and politically incorrect. Considering that was the daily reality that surrounded them, how then could they stick it out—stand strong—and make a difference?

JAMES 1:2–18

Consider it pure joy, my brothers, whenever you face trials of many kinds because you know that the testing of your faith develops perseverance. (James 1:2)

What a radical idea! Why on earth would we be thankful for problems and difficult circumstances? How could joy make an appearance as the result of trouble?

We find the first part of the answer in verses 3 and 4. We can't really know what perseverance is unless we experience things that try our faith. Then through the process of 'sticking it out', there develops a maturity that gives us a whole new perspective on what really matters in life. While it may be true that there is real work involved in maintaining a healthy faith, it is also true that having faith does not remove us from the hard and unpleasant things in life. In fact, having an active faith often seems to put us in the position of going through more of those tough things. Can we still regard faith as a gift in the face of these realities?

First, we need to see the joy James challenges us to have because it can literally surround all our hard places. We begin with the confidence we can have in the complete dependability of God—in or out of tough times. We can experience peace in the middle of every crisis because faith has settled our relationship with God and placed us in the position to have access to all the good things God offers through Christ. And finally, we can emerge on the other side of difficulty with the joy that comes from having found that God does indeed keep His promises.

The reality of crisis—either as a direct attack on what we believe or as a part of the circumstances in which we live—is inevitable. It is the difference God's gift of faith can make in crisis that makes our joy possible. Faith can act as a protection for us to effectively short-circuit some of the fears that hound us. Faith can also sustain us through the long-term cares and pressures of our lives. The real wonder of experiencing faith is that our supply cannot be used up—the more God meets our needs, the more aware we become of His inexhaustible resources.

The second part of the answer is given in verse 5 where James assures us that God will provide us with what we need to navigate the rough waters that sometimes surround us and break on the shore of life. All we have to do is allow God into the pitching boat of our circumstances and turn over the helm to Him. However, James cautions in verses 6-8 that when we ask, we must ask with the trusting confidence that God will indeed answer and provide what we need to meet the challenge that surrounds us—what it takes to persevere. He warns that not having faith when we pray, but instead regarding prayer as a last resort or emergency back-up plan will leave us in those rough waters with little hope of reaching the shore.

James goes on to further explain what he has said about persevering. In verses 9-11 he compares the way culture ranks a person's importance with the perspective we should have as Christians. Then he affirms once more in verse 12 the rich reward that sticking it out with God's help will bring. There is no comparison. Material possessions—no matter how attractive and valuable they may seem—can disappear in the blink of an eye, the richness of a relationship with God lasts for eternity.

There are many different kinds of 'trials' that we face, and in verses 13-15 James tackles the ever-present reality of temptation. His assurance is that when faced with this kind of trial, we can know that the nudging to do wrong has not come from God. He is not trying to trip us up. Our propensity to be enticed by these things and the desires that have the potential for damaging our lives and harming others comes from what is part of our own sinful nature. We can spray those all too common tendencies with weed-killer, or ignore them and let them grow into an invasive patch of weeds that takes over the whole garden.

While temptation is a fact of life for all of us, sinning is a choice. Once that choice to give in to temptation is made, the way is opened that leads us down a slippery slope of negative consequences. One bad decision leads to another and farther in the wrong direction, until the crevasse we have fallen into is too deep to escape on our own. However, when we identify temptation for what it is—an urging coming from our sinful human nature—we have the option and the opportunity to refuse to give it traction and to reject its enticement. *w/ stimulus from Satan*

Finally, James warns us in verses 16-18 not to lose sight of the fact that all we are and have comes from God. He is eternal and completely dependable. His Word declares how we can experience a new birth and know that He has created us with purpose and value.

Getting Personal...
Why Inside Out Matters

I grew up in a Christian home in which my mother and father enthusiastically lived out their faith and were very involved in our church by teaching, giving generously of themselves, and serving others in many different ways. When I was in first grade, I accepted Jesus as my Savior because I understood that he had died and risen again so my sins could be forgiven; and I knew that I wanted to be born again and be a part of God's family. So, I grew up being comfortable doing what was expected of a good girl in a Christian home. My faith was very real, but it had never been tested. Then the summer of my 14th year my whole world suddenly fell apart. My mother, who was also my dearest friend and whose companionship I enjoyed and took for granted, became very ill. My father had to take her to the hospital in the middle of the night, and it was several days before the doctors could pinpoint what was wrong. By the time the diagnosis was made, she could no longer breathe on her own and her condition worsened.

Those days were like a horrible nightmare for me. I couldn't believe what was happening. My prayers were frequent and desperate, and I was terrified of what might lie ahead. Then one night I did something I had never done before—I stopped telling God what I expected Him to do and instead put myself in His hands. I admitted I was frightened and didn't know how I was going to get through this. I cried out for His help. And there in that darkness, I experienced something that was totally unexpected— an amazing sense of peace that I had never felt before washed over me. Although I didn't fully understand what I felt, I had the assurance that God was with me and I knew I was not facing those devastating circumstances alone.

My mother only lived a few more days; but I discovered in the midst of all that pain and sorrow I still felt surrounded by God's presence and peace. Of course, I would never have chosen what had happened; but on the other side of it, I found that I had come to know God in a much deeper way than I had before. I learned that I could persevere in my faith because, though I am on a journey, I am not traveling alone. I discovered and have experienced many times since that God is always there to help me over the rough places in the road.

JAMES 1:19-27

"My dear brothers, take note of this: Everyone should be quick to listen, slow to speak, and slow to become angry, for man's anger does not bring about the righteous life God desires." (James 1:19)

As the old saying goes… 'the proof is in the pudding'. Likewise, the evidence of our saving faith in Christ is going to be seen—or 'tasted' - in how we live our daily lives. Even when we aren't thinking about it, others are very much aware of the flavor our words and actions have.

One of the very familiar stumbling blocks that trips us up in our relationships is anger. James' counsel is to take a deep breath, as it were, and think about our words before we open our mouths. What comes out of our mouths should reflect the relationship with have with God instead of opening the way to all kinds of sinful behaviors and painful consequences.

In verses 22-25, James uses an illustration—paints a word picture—of this important point he is making. Very simply, the truth that we take in should be reflected in what we do and say. His picture of looking in a mirror and then forgetting what we saw is a great example of the sort of distracted attention we've all experienced. But that's not how we should respond to God's Word. Instead, we are to read and interact with it by very intentionally studying what it says, absorbing its meaning, and following its teaching. No blank look in the mirror this time—rather the clear image of the blessing that comes with living out our faith.

In verses 26-27, just in case we have missed his main point, James reiterates how different mere politically correct 'religiosity' is from a sincere heart relationship with God. True religion—personally knowing God through Jesus—will be evident on the outside not only in what we say, but also in our tangible concern for others and our deliberate effort to avoid things that lead us in the wrong direction. Real faith isn't something we make a show of on the outside of our lives 'like an actor playing a role,' so we can look good to others. Instead, genuine faith comes from the inside because we have been born again and God's Spirit lives within us.

In this chapter James has written about several essential components that make it possible to 'stick it out' as Christians, even when life is difficult.

God doesn't tempt us—He allows us to be tested; but temptations come from our own sinful natures. We are assured that there is no difficulty which God cannot use to grow our faith. We can depend on God to help us—all we have to do is ask in faith, believing our prayer will be answered. Finally, James clearly states that God's values are very different from the materialistic values of our culture.

Therefore, when our inside-the-heart relationship with God is firmly grounded, we can stand strong, even when circumstances on the outside of our lives are challenging. Because of that reality, others won't be able to ignore the outside evidence—our words and actions—of the faith that lives within us.

Getting Personal... Why Inside Out Matters

Most of us, if we are truly honest, really don't like being told what to do or given a list of rules that we have to follow. There is deep within our human nature something that whispers, "Leave me alone—I'll do it my own way." Unfortunately, listening to that voice often has dire consequences.

Many years ago before the Communist regime took over China, a good friend of my father's was a missionary in China. Communist control forced his family to leave the country and the people to whom they had ministered for many years. They were thankful that even though one door had closed for them, they were able to plant a church in New York City's China Town and continue sharing the Gospel there.

One incident my father's friend described made a real impression on me and taught me an important truth. In the course of their ministry in China, he had met and witnessed to a man who was leading a very dangerous sort of life. He was, by his own admission, a 'professional thief' and evidently good at what he did, since he was not in jail. Although this very unlikely convert seemed to have been genuinely repentant for his sinful lifestyle and appeared to be serious about his Christian faith, the missionary had some real concerns. He imagined how difficult it must be for someone whose identity had been that of a law-breaker to completely leave that behind, even if he wanted to change.

The missionary decided it would be good to connect with this new believer to encourage him, and went to visit him at his home. When he arrived, he was warmly received. As he sat waiting for his host to bring in some tea, he noticed that on one wall of the room painted in large Chinese characters was the commandment, "Thou shalt not steal." The missionary's initial reaction affirmed what he had feared all along. Stealing was evidently a very hard temptation for this man to resist.

As the Chinese man walked back into the room, he notice the missionary staring at the words written on the wall. "Isn't that a wonderful thing," he joyfully said. "I don't have to steal anymore—there is a better way to live!"

That ex-thief hit the nail on the head! He had discovered what the rules God has given us in His Word are meant to do—lift us up and give us a new perspective on life so we are free to live life the best way possible.

How Do His Words Touch My Life?

What impact do you think James' letter would have had on its original recipients and the circumstances they may have faced?

How are his words especially relevant to us in our own cultural context? With what part of this chapter could you most identify? Why?

What do you think is the hardest piece of wisdom in this chapter to put into practice in your own life? Why?

What do you think James means in verses 9-10 about position and pride?

In verses 26 and 27 is James talking about a condition of our salvation or a result of it? How important is this final statement of the chapter?

WHAT DOES A LIFE CHANGED FROM THE INSIDE OUT LOOK LIKE?

Loving other people and seeing them as having the same intrinsic value as we have is not always the natural thing to do, even within the Body of Christ. One reason this is true is that society has always operated in such a way that some people end up with more power and prestige than others. Although the determining factors of that status may vary in different situations, the end result is always the same—a sliding scale is drawn by which one's worth and importance are arbitrarily measured and divisions occur.

That certainly was true in the first century when James wrote. Just from a secular perspective in Roman culture there was a wealthy landed aristocracy at the top above a proportionally small middle class. Below the middle class were those called 'plebes' who were economically impoverished, politically vulnerable, and in practical ways, often worse off than many slaves. A huge segment of the population (up to 50% in some places) were slaves and had no political or social freedoms. Even though many slaves were very well educated, they had lost their freedom because of Rome's iron-fisted control and military power.

Likewise, Jewish culture was also divided in both secular and religious ways with a wealthy and powerful upper class, including the ruling Temple establishment, while the largest segment of the population were farmers or tradesmen. However, although there were many Jews who were very poor, there were very few Jews who were slaves. Most of those who had either political or religious authority had achieved their status by alliances and compromises they had made with the Roman officials who controlled Israel.

Probably more significant in the Jewish culture of that time was whether one was a conservative Observant Jew for whom what the scriptures said was the rule of life and belief affecting every area of daily life, or a liberal Assimilated Jew who did not hesitate to compromise how he lived and worshipped in order to 'fit in' with Gentile ideas and customs. As you can imagine, there was a huge divide between these two perspectives on faith, ethnic heritage, and traditions. Perhaps even more divisive was the way one's spiritual status was perceived by how strictly and legalistically one kept the 'letter of the Law'. As Paul's perspective had been early in his spiritual journey, one's righteousness and standing in the religious community was primarily based on doing good works that focused on the outside of one's life, not the inside heart relationship with God.

Although we know from the book of Acts and Paul's epistles that there were those who had come to faith in Jesus from all national and religious groups and every level of society, for Christians the very fact of declaring their faith put them in yet another category that had the potential for changing the way others perceived them. In both Jewish and Roman culture, Christians were often looked at with suspicion as though they had somehow committed a sort of religious or cultural treason and violated the accepted norms. As the number of Christians continued to grow and as the Gospel was proclaimed from one end of the Roman Empire to the other, standing firm in one's faith sometimes became a matter of life or death, and the loving fellowship and support of other Christians could make a powerful difference for those who were struggling.

Certainly James had seen the kind of damage that being influenced by a social or religious hierarchy could bring to the body of believers to which he ministered in Jerusalem. His words of wisdom at the beginning of Chapter 2 directly address the potential damage favoritism can unleash and make a solid case for the kind of equality and brotherhood that should characterize a fellowship of Christians.

JAMES 2:1–13

*My brothers, as believers in our glorious Lord Jesus Christ, don't show favoritism.
(James 2:1)*

As James begins this part of his epistle, he comes directly to the issue that
needs to be addressed: Don't allow public opinion to influence the way we
treat others. Frequently, the first thing we notice about someone is the way
they are dressed, and all too often that determines the kind of welcome
they receive and whether or not we initiate a friendly conversation. (verses
2-3)

There is no softening James' assessment of such all too common behavior—
when we act that way we have been inexcusably judgmental. (verse 3)
How a relationship with Christ should change that sort of reaction may
be counter-cultural, but it has the power to transform a group of 'church
people' into the Body of Christ—a family of believers connected from
the inside out who are also ready and willing to welcome newcomers into
their fellowship. It isn't material wealth that determines whether or not we
experience the riches of God's grace and the fullness of His blessing. What
counts is faith—faith that's grounded on a solid heart relationship with
God—faith that comes from understanding God's love for us and shows
up in our lives because of our love for Him.

In verses 6-8, James poses a very basic questions: Aren't we trying to 'butter
up' the wrong people? In the first century, as it still often is today, it is those
who trade on their power or popularity who denigrate our Christian faith,
ridicule our beliefs, and often make life difficult. In many countries around
the world being a Christian puts one on the wrong side of the dictated
social and religious powers that be, and faith can mean persecution, prison,
and even death. Compromising our faith by this kind of favoritism to get
on the good side of the wrong people is not what we should be doing. Our
concern should be for those who are rich by God's reckoning.

When Jesus was asked what the most important part of the Law was, he
replied, *'Love the Lord your God with all your heart and with all your soul
and with all your mind.' This is the first and greatest commandment. And the
second is like it: 'Love your neighbor as yourself.' All the Law and the Prophets
hang on these two commandments. (Matt. 22:37-40)*

The two passages that Jesus quoted come from Deuteronomy 6:5 and Leviticus 19:18 and were considered to be a summation of the laws of the Old Testament. They were the most important requirements for living out a real, solid, inside-the-heart faith and were called the "Royal Law".

James points out that if we are not loving our neighbors in this way, we are doing some serious law-breaking. (verses 8-9) Once again, he goes back to the importance of not just looking religious by making sure others know we are checking off the 'Big Ten'. Rather, real, living faith is going to be demonstrated in the relationships we have with others. (verses 10-11) This kind of faith from the inside out is not easy. In fact, it really isn't possible unless it's a result of the other half of the Royal Law—the love we have for God.

In verses 12-13, James takes this principle one step further. As Christians who are commissioned to love others in this way, we will experience the freedom of extending mercy instead of being boxed-in by the effects of being judgmental. We can all too easily get caught up in a repeating cycle of fractured relationships when we allow a judgmental attitude to trump mercy as we relate to others. The opposite result comes from being willing to be merciful because we have received the blessing of God's mercy to us.

Getting Personal...
Why Inside Out Matters

Practice, competition, winning, getting the trophy—those are all an intrinsic part of team sports. It seems like our culture is so consumed with athletic competition that the pressure to win bragging rights is introduced to kids at a very young age.

When our son was in cub scouts, his troop entered a city-wide softball league. The dad who was coaching their team made sure they got lots of practice, and as the weeks passed their skill level really improved. However, he made it very clear both to the parents and the kids that playing softball was about more than winning. It was more important to learn to work together as a team and to be able to enjoy the game because they had worked hard and were ready to play.

The boys did much better than any of us expected for a first-year team, and good friendships were formed by those of us who enthusiastically watched the games. I was impressed with the positive way the coach helped them improve their skill level and how he encouraged them whether they were winning or not.

At the end of the season, their team had done well enough that they were in one of the play-off games against another team with a much different perspective on playing softball. That teams coach was very aggressive in the way he yelled instructions and criticized mistakes. Compared to what we were used to seeing in our son's team, the boys looked like they were feeling a lot of pressure to excel. The parents on the other side of the field also seemed to have a very competitive attitude toward the game.

Our son's team did very well—probably the best they had done all season. As the last inning began, they were just one point behind. After two outs, the bases were loaded and there was a good chance a solid hit would put them ahead. The batter up to the plate was a boy with Down syndrome who had been part of their troop all year. Although he had played enthusiastically all season, Matt had never hit a ball in a game. This time he picked up the bat, the pitcher threw the ball, he swung with all he had, and the sound of the impact resounded across the field.

The ball shot up in the air and dropped into the hands of the second baseman. Practically that was the end of the game—3rd out, no more runs, and the other team had its victory in the bag.

It was what happened next that I will always remember. While the other team was celebrating their win, there was even more excitement from our team as they all ran out on the field cheering, circling the boy Matt, jumping up and down, and giving him high-fives. He had hit the ball! All season they had hoped he'd do that—and now he had. Winning that play-off game and a trophy for their pack was nothing compared to Matt's success. That was really something to brag about and celebrate.

For us as parents, it was one of those moments that we would never forget. We were watching our sons care more about a special friend than whether or not they won a game. The truth was in the game of life lessons, they had won and won big.

JAMES 2:14–26

"What good is it, my brothers, if a man claims to have faith, but has no deeds? Can such faith save him?" (James 2:14)

Faith or works—which is more important? Can we choose one or the other and only focus on that? Does just saying I am a Christian cut it? Or is this question more complicated than that? James implies that it is a deeper question by using the word "such" to describe this kind of faith as being virtually undetectable to others looking from the outside.

This was a hot-button issue among Jewish (and Gentile) Christians in the first century and still remains front and center in religious discussions today. James begins his answer with a very clear example of what a verbal assent with no action to back it up looks like. (verses 15-16) The outside words are nice, but empty, because there is no connection to an inside heart conviction that would make a difference in the way life is lived on the outside.

In verses 17-19, James states very clearly that if faith is real—if it is not mere intellectual assent—it will be evidenced by our actions. It is not difficult for a person to say he believes in a 'higher power', that he is a monotheist, or that he believes there are 'spiritual forces' that affect us. Secular spirituality is a very popular thing in today's cultural environment. However, that sort of twisting of the truth has been something Satan has used since the beginning, and it is not the faith in Jesus as one's Lord and Savior that James is talking about.

James makes it clear that real from-the-heart faith is a very different thing. Martin Luther said that a man is justified (declared righteous before God) by faith alone; but not by a faith that is alone. In other words, genuine faith will produce good deeds. We can only be saved from our sin by accepting the redemption Jesus accomplished when he died and rose again; but when the inside is born again by that saving faith, the power of the transformation will be obvious in our words and actions on the outside. From the inside out makes all the difference in who we are and what we do.

In the section of this chapter that begins with verse 20, James gives two examples of faith in action from the Old Testament. The first example in verses 21-24 is Abraham—the patriarch of the Jewish people—a man chosen to enter into a Covenant with God (Gen. 12:1-3) that would impact not only his life, but the rest of history.

Abraham literally and spiritually began a journey when he entered into that Covenant relationship. It was a journey that would lead him to the land of Israel which would someday belong to his descendants, and a journey of trust and faith that would eventually identify him as a man of righteousness and describe him as God's friend. (Gen. 15:6; 2 Chron. 20:7) Neither journey was without bumps in the road and detours; but they both were journeys on which Abraham walked with God who was always there to get him back on track and encourage him. That journey eventually brought him to the place where his trust in God's promises and faithfulness was complete enough that he was willing to demonstrate what was on the inside by outwardly entrusting God with the life of his son. Given the history of the Jews, it is not surprising at all that James would use Abraham as an example of faith under construction that became a reminder to following generations of what real faith being lived out looks like. Abraham is considered the father of God's Chosen People, Israel—what better example could there be?

The second example, however, is one that might at first glance seem very unlikely. (verse 25) Why does James place Rahab the prostitute from Jericho alongside Abraham as a picture of genuine faith being lived out in the circumstances of life? There is no way to soften who Rahab was as a woman living in an army town on the margin of her society and part of a pagan and idolatrous culture. In Joshua 2 when we first meet Rahab, we find she has risked everything to provide a safe hiding place for two Israeli spies. Her action in this military citadel would have been considered treason, punishable by death. The text does not condone the lies she tells, but her deception demonstrates the length to which she was willing to go to protect the spies.

The first question we might ask about what she has done is, "why?". The answer can be found in the amazing statement of faith that she gave when she declared: I KNOW your God has given you this land, I KNOW your God dried up the Red Sea, I KNOW you destroyed the kingdoms of Sihon and Og, so THEREFORE...we are in great fear, our hearts are melting, and our courage has failed...BECAUSE..."The Lord your God is God in heaven above and on the earth below."

Although Rahab's faith was still in its infancy, it was solid enough for her to commit everything she was and had to its reality. She had the faith to believe that since she had chosen to declare her allegiance to the God of Israel by protecting the spies, she would receive His protection in return. Demonstrating her sincerity, not only did Rahab hide the spies and help them escape, but she also supplied them with a wise and safe plan to avoid capture.

If the story stopped here, it would be a powerful example of how having faith in who God is and His power can change a life... but this was not the end of Rahab's faith journey.

Rahab and her family were spared as the spies had promised, and became a part of the Israelite camp, first living "outside the camp" and then "among the Israelites". (Josh. 6:23-25) After she became part of the Israelite community, Rahab married Salmon who was a leader in the tribe of Judah and became the mother of Boaz, the husband of Ruth, and grandfather of David. Rahab is named along with Abraham as an example of inside-out faith because it transformed her life and was an example to others of the difference a relationship with God can make.

In conclusion, in verse 26 James sums up this section on the connection between faith and works. The outside can't exist without the inside; and if the inside is real, it can't help but transform the appearance on the outside so that it becomes obvious to those around us.

Getting Personal...
Why Inside Out Matters

When our daughter was in grade school, she and I went on a bus trip adventure to Chicago to spend a couple of days sight-seeing and so she could experience what being in a big city is like. We had a great time shopping at Marshall Fields, going to a musical, and visiting museums and other attractions, although I had the feeling she was a little overwhelmed by how different everything was from the much smaller town where we lived. When the trip was over, our plan was to take the commuter train from Chicago to Hammond where her grandparents lived and meet up with my husband and her younger brother.

She had never been on a train before and must have looked a bit unsure and hesitant about boarding. I was pleasantly surprised when the conductor noticed her hesitancy and took the initiative to greet her as he escorted us into the car. By the time we were getting close to Hammond, the train car was almost empty, since Hammond was near the end of the line. During the ride I had noticed how that same conductor seemed to go out of his way to be nice to people by answering questions, helping with packages, and just being friendly. His pleasant demeanor seemed to make this train ride quite different from what I had experienced on crowded commuter trains in the past.

As we neared our destination, my daughter leaned over and whispered, "He's so nice. Do you think he knows Jesus?" I was totally surprised by her question, which I figured must have come from a recent Sunday School lesson. Then I wondered if this might just be one of those 'teachable moments'.

As the train began to slow down and we stood up to gather our things so we could leave, the conductor asked if we had enjoyed being in Chicago. It must have been obvious we were on a trip and not commuters because of our suitcase and packages. My daughter enthusiastically began telling him about all we had seen and done and where we were headed now. As we were about to get off the train onto the platform, I did something sort of 'gutsy' and totally out of character for me. I told him how pleasant he had made our train ride, and then went on to say I had been wondering, and had to ask, if he was a Christian.

His answer was a big smile and a "yes". That's all the conversation we had because as soon as we stepped down from the train car we were being greeted by family and the train was leaving the station. But neither my daughter nor I forgot what he had said. So many times something has brought that train ride back to my mind, and I have been reminded how that conductor was living out his faith in a very natural way in the ordinary circumstances of his day. What's real on the inside does show up on the outside—even when we aren't consciously thinking about what we are doing or saying.

How Do His Words Touch My Life?

How hard is it to use God's standard in the way we treat people? What are the most common things that get in the way of seeing others as God does?

How did Jesus put this principle into action?

What are some of the ways people 'pick and choose' the things they do so others will look at them favorably?

How have you seen what verse 13 describes play out in situations you have been in?

How would you explain in your own words James' statements about the relationship of faith and works?

Why do you think James chose Abraham and Rahab as his examples of faith in action?

If you were going to select a contemporary example of this kind of dynamic faith, whom would you choose?

Why?

TACKLING SOME TOUGH TEMPTATIONS

Words that are spoken and the way they are said have always been a major component of how others perceive us and how relationships are built. Sometimes it may be the loudest voice that grabs our attention, or perhaps it is the words of the person who has the most recognizable name to whom we tend to listen. Money, power, fame, educational credentials, and charisma are all some of the factors that play into whose words we take seriously and whether or not we allow those words to impact us.

All through history, words have influenced people's lives and events—sometimes for good, but too often with the opposite effect. James fully understood the potential power that words can have. During his ministry, Jesus had often addressed this same issue. On more than one occasion, he pointed out the hypocrisy of religious leaders who said one thing, but did not follow their own teaching and put a spiritual stumbling block in the path of those they taught. (Matt. 23:1-4) Therefore, one of James' concerns was that those who were teaching others about what it means to have a relationship with God through Jesus were taking that responsibility seriously and that the source of their wisdom was God.

As Christians one of our fundamental beliefs is that God's Word is completely true and reliable. What God has said is the immutable standard on which the foundations of our faith is grounded and the moral standards by which our lives are measured. Twisting the truth, adding our own 'creative' interpretations, or picking and choosing what parts of scripture we want to follow are simply not options if we are going to have a genuine inside-the-heart relationship with God.

The religious climate of the first century had the potential for creating such conflicting doctrines and fostering false teachings. Hanging on to some of the views held by the various sects of Judaism could create a divisive environment between Christians, particularly in drawing lines between Jewish and Gentile believers. At the time of Jesus and James there were some Jewish leaders like the Herodians who took an almost secular view of scripture and were much more concerned with political power than issues of faith. The Sadducees were one of the very influential religious factions and were made up primarily of rich and high priestly families who were in charge of the Temple and its services. In doctrinal matters, they held a very limited view of scripture, only accepting the Pentateuch, denying life after death, the existence of angels and demons, and that God was concerned with how people actually lived their lives as long as they observed the ritualistic laws of Levitical purity. Because of their wealth and position, their primary concern was to protect the status quo so that nothing would threaten their tenuous relationship with the Roman authorities who controlled Israel.

At the other end of the spectrum were the Pharisees who generally controlled the synagogues and whose teachings strongly influenced the general population. Pharisees were passionate about knowing and obeying scripture, and their primary emphasis was on the importance of keeping the Law. Over the years in their zealous effort to make sure no law in the Torah was broken, they had added a huge number of their own oral laws and traditions that affected virtually every area of life. Though the original intent of these rules had been to create a "fence" to protect the sacred Law of scripture, instead, over time they had become a heavy burden of rules that were almost impossible for people to keep.

Jesus had over and over again focused on the importance of not only knowing the words of the Law, but actually allowing the spirit of the Law to make a difference in the way one lived. Once again, it's the inside—the heart relationship with God—that will make what happens on the outside not just struggling with rote legalistic obedience, but instead discovering the joy of living life the best way possible—the way God intended.

In this third chapter of his epistle, James considers two closely related and critically important subjects: The damage that can be done by an unchecked tongue and the danger of a spiritually unhealthy doctrine masquerading as wisdom. What is taught and spoken, if it is not true and wholesome, can spread harmful consequences like a cancer. Empty philosophies, twisted truth, and blatant falsehoods can destroy individual lives and ruin relationships. The names attached to those perpetrating this sort of false teaching may have changed over the centuries since James wrote, but the potential danger they can cause remains the same.

JAMES 3:1–12

Not many of you should presume to be teachers, my brothers, because you know that we who teach will be judged more strictly. We all stumble in many ways. If anyone is never at fault in what he says, he is a perfect man, able to keep his whole body in check. (James 3:1-2)

James certainly knew and had seen how the false and twisted teachings of the various Jewish sects had affected the people of his own day. His warning is that when a prideful manipulation of scripture to accomplish one's own agenda works its way into Christian doctrine and practice, it will result in factions between believers and a skewed view of leadership. From the "religion is really not that important" view of the politically minded Herodians, to the very liberal "get all you can right now" mantra of the Sadducees, to the legalistic "follow all the rules" dogma of the Pharisees, Jewish Christians in the first century were surrounded by a wide range of conflicting world views. Unfortunately it was possible for faith in Jesus as the Messiah—the fulfillment of all the Old Testament had taught and promised (Matt. 5:17)—to be distorted by trying to work some of those lingering sectarian concepts into the mix.

Thus James' concern is that those who teach have the responsibility to be sure both the content of what they teach and how they communicate it meet God's standards of truth and wisdom. In any context, a teacher is not qualified to teach unless he thoroughly knows the subject matter. Going a step farther, knowing the subject matter—especially in the case of teaching the message of salvation and how to live life God's way—means more than rote memorization of an outline or text. It requires having come to know what faith in Jesus means because one has experienced it personally on the inside. We can only teach with honesty and conviction if our outside words come from an inside relationship with Jesus. Without that crucial connection, it is almost certain things will go the wrong way.

The first thing James emphasizes is that being a teacher—especially a teacher within the Body of Christ—carries with it a very serious commitment to live a life characterized by wholesomeness and integrity. How can a teacher expect to be respected and taken seriously if he is not demonstrating what he has taught by what he says and does?

Of course, James knows that none of us can live without "stumbling". Even if absolute perfection may not be humanly possible, he specifically identifies an aspect of the way we interact with others in which we ought to invest very deliberate effort and discipline. What comes out of our mouths can literally make us or break us and is often the primary way we are initially judged by others.

Parables are word pictures that give tangible examples of an important truth. Jesus frequently used parables to explain and illustrate the concepts he was teaching; and in the next several verses James paints some word pictures of his own to drive home what he is saying about the effect words can have and how necessary it is to control them. He uses horses, ships, forest fires, and taming wild animals to reinforce the point he is making. Although the tongue may seem inconsequential when compared with other parts of our bodies, controlling it is vitally important.

In verses 6 and 8, James lists some of the ways an unchecked tongue can cause damage and makes the somewhat discouraging statement that on our own we really can't control it. No matter how much we think we know or how well we are expressing it, teaching or sharing God's truth is a calling and ministry that we can't take lightly.

Continuing in verses 9 through 12, James describes the damaging words and hypocrisy that can pour out of our mouths. Very simply, this should not be how it is! Talking out of both sides of our mouths on the outside reveals the lack of a solid spiritual commitment in our hearts. How can we claim to have real inside faith if the verbal evidence of that faith is sorely lacking? Again James uses word pictures to make his point. Does a fresh water spring produce salt water? Do olives show up on fig trees or figs on grapevines? Of course not. So how can we reconcile or excuse both pious and profane words coming out of our mouths if we claim to have been transformed—born again—on the inside? What's missing if our tongues aren't tamed and we find ourselves stumbling over our words? How can we surmount such a prevailing and daunting problem?

Getting Personal...
Why Inside Out Matters

It was a beautiful late summer morning—sunshine, birds singing, a pleasant breeze. Our yard backs up to a bike trail; and on the other side of the trail there is a high berm covered in wild flowers, tall grass, and trees that obscure a busy highway. Since we built our house several years ago, the trees have grown so tall that one wouldn't even know the highway was there unless there was unusually loud traffic noise.

I had just taken some folded laundry upstairs and happened to glance out a window facing the trail. Surprised to see some smoke rising from the other side of the berm some distance away near an intersection, I tried to see where the smoke might be coming from. I couldn't tell, but what had been just a wisp a few minutes before had suddenly become a large plume of dark smoke.

Realizing that the berm itself must be on fire, I grabbed the closest phone and called 911. Then I ran downstairs, hurried out into the yard, turned on the hose, and started spraying the vegetation behind our fence, hoping the fire wouldn't come this far.

It seemed like I heard sirens almost as soon as I got outside; but in the few minutes it took the firemen to begin attacking the fire, it had spread down the berm almost as far as our house. Thankfully, by coming at it from all directions the fire crew was able to keep the fire away from the houses along the trail, but I was amazed at how quickly the flames—encouraged by that breeze that had earlier seemed so pleasant—raced down both sides of the berm. By the time the fire was contained, it had devoured about a mile of vegetation and could have done a lot more damage if it hadn't been stopped so quickly.

That night there were pictures on the local news of the fire and what it had done. The fire chief said it was probably started by a cigarette thrown from a car window. Such a tiny spark tossed away with no thought of what the consequences might be… what a powerful picture of how carelessly spoken words can incinerate relationships.

JAMES 3:13-18

Who is wise and understanding among you? Let him show it by his good life, by deeds done in humility that comes from wisdom. (James 3:13)

The solution to this very familiar and all too common reality that James has described in the first part of this chapter is wisdom. But he is not talking about just any wisdom. This wisdom is the kind that comes from knowing God and seeing life as a journey of faith on which He walks with us. Because we know that the wisdom God gives does not come from our own intellectual accomplishment, we can understand that it is a gift from God Himself. It is not just acquired information, but rather practical insight—truth from an inside-the-heart relationship with God—that has real-time spiritual implications for what we do and say. Humility is the hallmark of such wisdom because its source is knowing God through the salvation Jesus has made possible and the inside new birth we have experienced.

James also provides a clear description of the wrong kind of wisdom and the damage it can do. (verses 13-16) Since the source of that wisdom comes from our confidence in our own accomplishments, there is a man-made rating scale that accompanies it. That attitude quickly opens the door to pride, envy, and selfish ambition. Relying on the shaky foundation achieved by our own ambitions so that others will perceive us as "wise" and we will win popular approval can quickly lead to behaviors like boasting and twisting the truth. The false and divisive teachings that gain traction when we are pursuing our own agenda can have tragic consequences in both spiritual and relational ways.

In contrast (verses 17-18), the wisdom that God provides is as different as night and day. Foundationally, it is completely true and right and is the result of our relationship to God. It's "inside" wisdom that bursts forth on the outside and enables us to be "peace-loving, considerate, submissive, full of mercy and good fruit, impartial and sincere." What an impossible list of attributes that should characterize us if we are trying to gain them on our own! But when it's God who is teaching and empowering us so that we will be able help and instruct others in their faith journeys, the evidence of real wisdom can become part of who we are in Christ.

One of the circumstances that occasionally arose in the Christian fellowships of James' day was that of someone trying to redefine, water-down, or add to the gospel message to fit his own agenda. As we have already noted, those misguided false teachers had been part of or influenced by the teachings of one of the Jewish sects and still hung on to things like earning favor with God by good works as a requirement of salvation. Another common bending of the truth emphasized that head knowledge or a verbal statement of belief in Jesus was essentially all that mattered. There have been other directions that faulty wisdom has taken over time, but all the different variations have had the same result—diminishing the importance of an inside the heart commitment to Jesus as Savior and Lord by trying to combine that simple and essential faith with man-made dogma masquerading as wisdom.

James concludes this chapter on teaching and wisdom (verse 18) with another word picture, one that seems to echo what Jesus taught. When godly wisdom grows from an inside faith to outside words and actions, it will create a dynamic sense of Christian community and encourage an environment in which living out one's faith bears bountiful fruit.

A word about the book of
JAMES AND THE OLD TESTAMENT BOOK OF PROVERBS

The book of Proverbs is all about what godly wisdom looks like (2:1-5) and how to walk with God through all the hills and valleys of life (15:33; 16:3). It deals in a very down-to-earth and practical way with how to live a life that comes from an inside relationship with God. It was meant to be a teaching tool—a way to learn and understand the differences in everyday life that having that heart commitment with God would make. Most of the proverbs are short and easy to remember and frequently use a word picture to illustrate the concept being taught.

There are several places in the letter James wrote to those Jewish Christians of the first century that sound very similar to the book of Proverbs. This style of writing would have had a familiar feel for the initial recipients of James' epistle and is one of the stylistic elements that gives his writing a very Jewish flavor.

While this kind of writing may not be as common in the literature of our own culture, it still speaks with clarity and practicality. Truth is truth. God's wisdom about living life the best way possible does not change. The evidence is clear that inside faith lived on the outside is still as powerful today as it has been since the beginning.

Getting Personal...
Why Inside Out Matters

Unfortunately, it seems people in our modern secular culture are more easily drawn to charismatic 'spiritualists' and the cults they represent than one might expect. In the 'new age' era of the early 70's there was a fairly young nature-worshiping Indian guru who was attracting quite a following and had recently made Denver his spiritual headquarters.

The way that college students, in particular, were embracing his philosophy was very unsettling to watch. On one occasion, I happened to be picking someone up at the Denver airport at the same time a flight he was on arrived. As he walked into the terminal with his entourage, a large crowd of young people waiting in the concourse fell to their knees and bowed before him as he passed. I could hardly believe my eyes!

Since we were in youth ministry then, we were quite concerned about this man's popularity and all the publicity this cultic group was getting in the media. His appeal seemed to be centered on a 'feel-good-let's-all-get-along-be-one-with-nature' mantra that not only involved things like ritual meditation but was often connected to the use of drugs. At that time and place, it all this seemed to appear very hip and cool to a lot of people.

As spring break drew closer that year, the news reported that this guru and his followers were going up on a mountain for a couple of days to celebrate the changing of seasons and to worship the sun. It was very disturbing to see all the publicity this cult was getting, and we had real concerns that some of the kids we worked with might be attracted to this group.

At the same time all this was taking place, we met with a group of other Christians with whom we regularly prayed. That particular evening, our prayers were focused on the false teaching that this cult and its leaders were promoting. We specifically prayed for God to protect the kids in our youth group from these pagan beliefs. Then we prayed for God to make it very clear what was true and what was false so that people would see this cult for what it really was.

The answer to our prayers was almost immediate and more dramatic than we could have ever imagined. In fact, the would-be sun worshippers didn't even get to see the sun at all. The very night after they had hiked up to the place where they planned to worship the sun, a spring blizzard arrived with a vengeance. When the storm subsided, the cold and wet sun worshippers and their humiliated leader had to be rescued by the National Guard and transported down the mountain. The facade the cult and its false teaching had built virtually melted, away leaving only muddy puddles of disillusionment.

However, the Son we worship who is revealed to us through the wisdom that comes from God's Word and the heart relationship we have with Him remains the eternal Light of the World. God's truth wins every time.

How Do His Words Touch My Life?

Why does James single out teaching as an area of caution?

What's the broader principle here that also applies to other areas of giftedness and service?

Why is what we say such a barometer of who we are?

What examples have you seen of damage done by the wrong words used in the wrong way—either deliberately or accidentally spoken?

Are there religious groups today that have led people in the wrong direction by changing the message of the gospel in some way?

Curses and blessings—why is James so emphatic about this?

How can one live wisely? Humbly? How would you put verse 13 into your own words?

Is there a disconnect between the values our culture holds and what James says about faulty wisdom?

James addresses two hard areas of discipleship—speaking and thinking. Why do you think these two aspects of the Christian life are so important?

Why are they often overlooked or avoided?

Look at Psalm 19:14. How does this passage affirm what James has written?

THE IMPORTANCE OF GIVING GOD CONTROL

In the first three chapters of his epistle James has over and over again emphasized how vitally important it is to have an inside heart relationship with God made possible by the salvation Jesus offers. He has also made it clear that when we have entered into that genuine heart relationship with God, the outside evidence of our commitment should be obvious to others in how we talk and what we do.

Even when both of those things are a reality—the inside faith and the outside deeds—we will still continue to be faced with temptations and decisions that have the potential for pulling us in the wrong direction. Being a Christian—having our sins forgiven and our guilt removed—does not mean that we will no longer be confronted with choices that need to be made; nor does it mean it will always be easy to choose to do the right thing.

We have previously compared the relationship we have with God to a faith journey or walk. That image is often used in both the Old and New Testaments and provides a word picture that is very easy to visualize.

The journey begins when we stand at a fork in the road and make the deliberate life-changing decision to leave the path we've made for ourselves and step into the way God has shown us. Walking with someone is a very natural way to get to know them better—to have conversations—to learn more about who they are—to build a very comfortable and enjoyable friendship. The more often we walk and the farther we go, the relationship we have becomes deeper and more important to us than how far we've walked or merely going through an exercise routine. God knows the path; and even when it's steep or rocky or goes through unfamiliar territory, we can be confident that He will be there, walking along side us and showing us the way. As C.S. Lewis describes in the Narnia books, in one's experience of coming to know God, the "farther up and further in" we go, the more "solid" and beautiful our surroundings become until the path eventually leads us into God's eternal presence.

So if that's what walking with God is like because of the faith we have on the inside, what could possibly happen that isn't good? The unfortunate reality is that a lot can go wrong, not because God deserts us and we are left on the path alone, but because we get distracted and wander off the path into the underbrush. The bad news is that when we step off the path, we can trip over rocks, get scratched up by thorns, or stung by nasty bugs. The good news, however, is that God will always be waiting for us to realize our detour wasn't the best idea and will help us step over the rocks, away from the thorns and bugs, and get us back on track.

In this fourth chapter, James' focus is on some of those things that grab our attention and end up having a negative effect on our relationship with God, how we live out our lives, and our interactions with others. Temptation is very real and comes in many different sizes and shapes. Allowing God to have control in those tempting situations that so frequently arise makes all the difference. He's the one who wrote the guide book and knows how the GPS (God's Perfect Steps) works; so asking for His help in navigating bumps in the road and staying on course will make the walk a lot more enjoyable.

JAMES 4:1–6

What causes fights and quarrels among you? Don't they come from your desires that battle within you? (James 4:1)

When things are not quite right on the inside, one of the first places that a problem surfaces is in relationships. The example James uses is the very common dissatisfaction that comes from wanting something we don't have. Whether what we desire is something tangible like money or possessions, or something harder to pin down like popularity or power, once we allow obtaining it to become a priority, we will find ourselves off the path and stumbling around in the weeds. Coveting whatever has become an obsession will stir up the kind of jealously and eventually hatred that kills relationships. The way we treat others can easily become very contentious and manipulative. Getting what we think we have to have takes over and skews our perception of what really matters in life.

In verse 3, James zeroes in on what the real inside-the-heart issue often is: Whatever this consuming desire is, we are pursuing it on our own. We have lost sight of the spiritual truth that God is the giver of all good gifts. In contrast, when we allow Him to be in control—when we stay on the path beside Him—He will provide us with what is truly essential. But that isn't all. When we are walking with Him, He will also create within our hearts the very desires that will bring a tangible awareness of fullness and blessing into our lives. There is a profound difference between expecting God to give us everything we ask for and having a deepening relationship and dependence on Him. When we have that inside-the-heart relationship, we can trust God to shape within us the wisdom to know what we really need to become complete—to be all that He created us to be.

In verses 4 and 5, James uses an illustration of how off-track we can get if we allow a worldly mindset to become what drives us. We have to make our choice and be committed to it. We can't have it both ways; either we are a friend of God and walking life's path with Him, or we betray that friendship by leaving the path to follow someone going in the opposite direction. James adds a word of encouragement in verse 6 as he reminds us that God certainly knows and understands our weakness and tendency to envy; but God is also the giver of grace to all who will receive it when those temptations arise.

Getting Personal...
Why Inside Out Matters

When our son was in high school, he made the decision to let his hair grow long. While that style might not have been our first choice as parents, we really didn't have a problem accepting it. He always pulled it back neatly in a pony tail, and I have to admit, I thought it actually looked good on him.

Maybe one of the reasons his choice didn't bother me was because it was not done as an act of rebellion, but was simply the way he had decided to manage his hair, which had always been less than cooperative. I was proud of him in so many ways. He was a young man of character who studied hard, gave his best to football and soccer, and was very serious about living out his faith as a Christian.

The last week of his junior year, I was making the rounds of classrooms for teacher conferences. When I came to the band room to talk to the director of the jazz band in which my son had really enjoyed participating, his teacher gave me the sort of 'good student' report I expected. Then he said, "I have to tell you something about your son that I am really ashamed to admit." Of course, all my mother alarms went off. I couldn't imagine what he was going to say; and what he did say was certainly not what I had expected.

He told me that when my son had come to audition for the jazz band, he had immediately judged what sort of kid he must be—all because of the long hair. My son had played well enough to get into the band, but the director had still wondered if he would be 'trouble'. However, what he had discovered was that this was not just a long-haired kid who could play the guitar—he was someone who practiced faithfully, was very dependable and responsible, and was a whole lot of fun to be around.

What an example of why not to judge others by a first impression based on appearance! I was really impacted by that band director's very honest admission that he had made a mistake in stereotyping my son. That incident has often served to remind me that I have to be careful not to make the same sort of snap judgment—even when it is tempting.

JAMES 4:7–16

Submit yourselves then to God. Resist the devil, and he will flee from you. Come near to God and He will come near to you. (James 4:7)

There is a much better alternative we can choose to prevent ourselves from being enticed off the path by allowing worldly values and priorities to take over thoughts and actions. In verses 7-10, James presents a very clear plan of attack that will make a tremendous difference in the way we handle the temptations with which we are faced. He makes it plain that there is nothing passive about what needs to happen. First, we must submit ourselves to God, taking the very deliberate step of giving God the control of our lives—what we think, and say, and do. Secondly, we must take another step in the right direction by saying a definite "no" to Satan and his attempts to detour our faith.

What will submitting to God and resisting Satan require of us? We are going to have to clean up our lives and get rid of any kind of impurity that has dirtied the corners of our minds and hearts. Then there needs to be a genuine repentance—real sorrow—for whatever sinful thoughts or actions or words that we've turned a blind eye to and accepted as okay, or as a social norm. Finally, we have to embrace a true humility before God, recognizing Him as our Lord and Savior and the only One who knows this path we have chosen to walk in fellowship with Him.

The differences those inside-the-heart choices make will be powerful. Satan will be forced to head in the other direction. God will walk closely by our side. We will experience the kind of fullness of life only God can provide.

Submission may be the solution to being distracted and tripped up as we walk with God, but it is not always an easy mindset for us to maintain. In verses 11 and 12, James points out another problem area we need to avoid: The slippery slope caused by thinking we have 'made it' spiritually and becoming judgmental of others. Just as it was common in the religious Jewish culture of James' time, ritualistic rule-keeping, doing good deeds for selfish reasons, and perceiving others as less spiritual than we are can lead very quickly to a "holier than thou" attitude and judging. James reminds us that there is only one Judge and the laws we are using are His. We will be held accountable to the same standard that we have hijacked to compare ourselves with others and judge them.

Another way we can get out of step is by thinking we have some sort of control of the future. Because of placing our confidence in what we have or what we have accomplished, we can easily fall into the trap of believing we can not only plan our future, but can also make those plans happen. In verses 13-16, James emphasizes how foolish that kind of self assurance is. The truth is that we have no control over the events that lie ahead. Of course we can wisely set realistic goals and lay out a plan for achieving them, but we need to keep in mind, with humility, that the future is not in our hands. Part of our inside-the-heart relationship with God is being able to trust Him enough so that we don't have to worry about manipulating situations and events to accomplish what we have outlined as our own agenda. With another word picture James reminds us that, compared to God, we are no more powerful than a wisp of fog.

He not only makes the point that assuming we have set the course for our future and bragging about the ingenuity of our plan is someplace we should not go, he also releases us from the burdensome misconception of believing we do have some control of future events. We are walking along this path of faith with God beside us. He fully knows what is around each bend in the road and over each hill, and He will make certain we have all we need for the journey. Using this faith journey word picture, we might compare the difference between putting the future in God's hands and trying to control it ourselves to planning a road trip without a map through a foreign country whose language we don't understand, or taking a tour with full amenities under the guidance of the person who had laid out and built the roads.

Getting Personal...
Why Inside Out Matters

There was absolutely no warning that a flood was coming. Headed from Iowa to Colorado to speak at a retreat, we were impatient to put this piece of western Nebraska behind us. As the monotonous gray ribbon of Interstate 80 stretched endlessly ahead, the rhythmic hum of tires on blacktop provided a fitting accompaniment for the gray boredom of the morning.

Then came the startling staccato of rain on the windshield and in the moment it took to turn on the wipers, morning had slipped back into twilight. A gust of wind slammed into the car and the deafening roar of rushing water burst upon us with the suddenness of a thunder crack. Before one mile sign had yielded to the next, a trickle of water in the ditch had risen to the level of the pavement. In the time it took to ease the car to the shoulder, we could no longer tell where the four lanes of interstate ended and the nearby Platte River began. Horrified, we watched the car ahead of us float off the road (as if in slow motion) and come to rest nose down against the pier of an overpass.

What five minutes before had been four lanes of highway through drought-parched farmland was now a vast expanse of turbulent brown. There was nothing but water as far as we could see—dark, churning, rushing, swirling water. The heavy, earthy smell of mud hung in an eerie stillness that was only broken now and again by the splintering of uprooted trees crashing into 18-wheelers marooned like angular islands caught in this unnatural sea. In the distance we, heard the first wail of a siren.

Without warning, life can totally change in a moment. What once seems as familiar and ordinary as driving through Nebraska can suddenly be gone, and we find ourselves facing circumstances we could not have anticipated and for which we are completely unprepared.

The reality is, we aren't able to know or control what the future holds. But we can have the absolute confidence that God does, and He has promised to provide what we need to get through whatever comes our way. Life can be like a flash flood, but God is the solid Rock we can stand on so the waters can't reach us.

JAMES 4:17

Anyone, then, who knows the good he ought to do and doesn't do it, sins. (James 4:17)

What an incredibly powerful summation of one of the most important truths James' epistle emphasizes over and over again! This is one of the strongest definitions of sin in the Bible. Sin can be defined as deliberate rebellion against God and knowingly breaking the laws He has given. It can also be described as "missing the mark" like an arrow not very carefully aimed at a target. In this description of sin, James raises the bar even higher than those more familiar definitions by saying that we sin whenever we know the right thing to do or say, but choose instead not to do it. Even if whatever we have committed or omitted seems trivial or inconsequential, it is significant because we have made a choice. We knew what the right thing was, and even if no one else was aware or not, we chose to let it slide.

The closer we walk with God along the path of life, the deeper our inside-the-heart relationship to Him will grow, and the more finely tuned our sense of right and wrong will become. When that is true, as our spiritual walk continues, there will be more and more outside evidence of that inside faith.

Getting Personal... Why Inside Out Matters

One ordinary Sunday morning in December, I left my purse, in the K-1 Sunday School room while all of the kids and adult leaders went upstairs for our large-group worship and teaching time. I had done that for more than ten years and didn't give it a second thought. It wasn't until I had gotten home later and opened my purse, that I discovered my wallet was gone. What a horrible feeling!

I looked every place I could think of and retraced my steps—more than once—but it had simply vanished. It was gut-wrenching enough to have had my wallet stolen, but even more disturbing to have it happen while I was at church, the place that had always seemed so safe. (Since then I have learned that, just because of the high level of trust people tend to have, churches are an easy target for thieve, especially around Christmas time.)

I did all the things one has to do: Reported it to the police, got a new driver's license and insurance cards, and cancelled credit cards. Because of what had happened, after that we started a new protocol on Sunday mornings and locked up our purses before leaving the room to go upstairs. In fact, I started locking my new billfold in my car before I went into the building.

I kept hoping it would show up, but as the months passed, I gave up all hope of ever seeing it again and eventually almost forgot what had happened.

One Saturday morning the next spring, just when the snow had melted and the weather had finally gotten nice, I got a phone call. It was from a man who said he was out looking for mushrooms in a wooded area near a lake a few miles away. He asked what my name was, and then told me he had just found my wallet under a pile of soggy brush in the woods near a bike trail.

I was blown away! How did it get there? How on earth did he happen to find it in such a remote spot? We quickly arranged a place to meet near where he was, and I drove out to the lake, still in a state of disbelief.

The wallet was soaked and muddy and full of bugs, but the credit cards were still there along with the other things, like my driver's license. Only the cash was gone.

The man who had called me was probably in his mid-twenties, dressed for a mushroom hunt in the muddy woods, and seemed very glad he was able to return the billfold to me. I thanked him several times and asked for his address so I could write to thank him more formally.

As we were ending our conversation, he said something I will never forget. With a slightly self-conscious smile he said, "I couldn't have done anything else; it was just the right thing to do." Oh, but he could have done something else: Let it stay where he had found it, tried to use the credit cards, or simply thrown it in the trash. No one else would have ever known. Instead, he made the very deliberate effort to do the right thing because he knew in his heart of hearts what that right thing was.

How Do His Words Touch My Life?

What types of sins does James particularly single out in this chapter and why are they so potentially harmful?

Is there anything in this chapter that strikes you as being very similar to what confronts us in our own culture?

The Message version paraphrases verses 7-10 in this way:

So let God work his will in you. Yell a loud no to the Devil and watch him scamper. Say a quiet yes to God and he'll be there in no time. Quit dabbling in sin. Purify your inner life. Quit playing the field. Hit bottom, and cry your eyes out. The fun and games are over. Get serious, really serious. Get down on your knees before the Master; it's the only way you'll get on your feet.

What choice has to be made to get back on track?

What are the steps James lists that must be taken?

What part of his instruction seems to you to be the most difficult? Why?

When we put ourselves in a position of judgment we are making an affront to God and His Word. Why?

In the Old Testament God's relationship to Israel is often pictured as a marriage, and God's love for His people is described as being both zealous and jealous. Israel's sin and willfully turning away from God is called spiritually adultery. Why is the image of sin as adultery such a powerful word picture?

How would you define sin?

What makes something "sinful"?

In what ways to you think one's definition of sin might change the longer one is a Christian?

HOW THEN SHOULD WE LIVE?

As James has explained and illustrated throughout his epistle, entering into a heart relationship with God involves a life-changing choice: Making a deliberate and solid commitment of faith inside the heart that is then evident outside by the things we do and the words we say. Making that choice is the most important decision of our lives and living it out is the most significant thing we will ever do. However, it is something we cannot successfully accomplish on our own. The inside-the-heart salvation is only possible because of the price Jesus paid for our sin and the forgiveness God's loving grace pours into our lives. We cannot earn that inside-the-heart relationship with God, nor can we manufacture an outside veneer of righteousness that will change the inside. Being born again is entirely God's doing. When our hearts are filled with the presence of God's spirit, the proof of that reality will spill over in every part of our lives.

Becoming a Christian is a decision we have to take very seriously because it will impact everything in the present and in the future. First, we have to admit that our lives have been bent and broken by sin and we cannot fix the problem ourselves. Then we must believe that the salvation Jesus accomplished on the cross by his death and resurrection is the only viable solution to meet our spiritual need. Finally, we have to commit ourselves to accept this life-changing relationship with God that Jesus offers, and willingly place the control of the inside and outside of who we are into His hands.

The original recipients of James' letter certainly needed to understand those truths to meet the challenges of being a Christian in the 1st century, and the same is true for us today. It seems that there is no end to the thoughts and situations that bombard us and can get in the way of that vital sync between the inside commitment and outside words and actions. James has addressed many of those very real things we may face and has offered encouragement, wise counsel, and practical advice on how to confront them—not on our own, but with the power of God's spirit in our lives. In this final chapter of his letter, James continues to write about some serious problems which we may encounter that could have a disastrous effect on both our personal faith and our relationships with other believers. Finally, he concludes with some very important and practical encouragement that will help the Body of Christ thrive and grow.

JAMES 5:1–6

Now listen, you rich people, weep and wail because of the misery that is coming upon you. (James 5:1)

Money and possessions have always been a point of contention in virtually every cultural context. James has already addressed some of the problems wealth and a desire to have it can cause. Favoritism and deference is often given to those who are well-off (2:1-4), and James reminds us that those things should not be part of our perspective. Not only should we have a giving heart toward the poor, but we should realize that true riches come from the faith relationship we have with God. Envying others and coveting what we don't have also has the potential for doing us serious relational and spiritual harm. (4:1-3)

In both of those instances, James seems to be describing temptations and attitudes that can side-track us as Christians, but in verses 1-6 of this chapter, he seems to be addressing those outside the fellowship of believers. The warning and call to repentance he gives are very similar to the warnings of the Old Testament prophets. He uses powerful language and vivid descriptions both to admonish those whose goal is wealth and power and to urge them to repent. At the end of one's life it is not how much money one has accumulated that matters; it's how one has lived out his life. Dishonesty, a lack of integrity, and the disparaging and unfair treatment of others will eventually become known and will be judged. All the financial clout and material things that brokered a false sense of security will in the end amount to nothing and be virtually worthless. Pursuing luxury and self-indulgence will prove to have been wasted effort and will fade away like a bad dream. James' assessment of the futility of an obsession with wealth is strong and to the point, but it is important to note that he begins it with a plea to change. Repentance is always an option, even for the self-centered rich, because the message of scripture is that any life can be transformed from the inside out by accepting the salvation Jesus offers.

From our own recent history, one graphic example of wrong choices and priorities is Saddam Hussein. An inflated ego, obsessive power, self aggrandizement, a disregard for the value of life, and an obscenely opulent lifestyle were what defined him. But when his self-indulgent and corrupt world fell apart, where did his life end? He met his death hiding in a hole in the ground with nothing remaining of his wealth or power, and will be remembered as one of the most evil and cruel men who has ever lived.

Another contemporary example with the opposite outcome, is Chuck Colson. His rise to power, influence, and all the trappings that went with his position were the result of his involvement in corrupt political schemes and calculated dishonesty. However, his story has a much different ending. Around the same time he was confronted with his crimes and sentenced to time in prison as a Watergate felon, Colson was also presented with the gospel message and how a relationship with Jesus could transform his life. Convicted of his sin, he repented and made that commitment. When he was released from prison, he began Prison Fellowship Ministry, which reaches out to those who are incarcerated and desperately need to hear about God's love and the forgiveness that can make a new life possible. Because of his passion for sharing how that inside-the-heart faith can make a difference in what happens on the outside, Colson became a respected and influential evangelical leader working to present the Christian world view to our culture. Since his death, the far-reaching legacy of his faith continues to make a difference and impact individual lives and the culture in which we live. What a powerful contemporary picture of what James wrote!

Getting Personal...
Why Inside Out Matters

When my husband and I were in youth ministry, settling into our first church in Denver, and trying to establish a good rapport with the youth groups, we received an invitation to attend the monthly potluck luncheon meeting of the Dorcas Circle. We almost didn't go, thinking that surely this group of rather elderly ladies had only asked us out of a feeling of obligation because we were new to Colorado and their church. We were afraid that all of us would experience severe generation-gapitis and mutual boredom.

How wrong we were! Not only were we served delicious food that reminded us of home, but we began to get to know some of the most delightful Christians we had ever met. Some of the Dorcas ladies came from tough pioneer stock, and others were from "back East", but they were all bound together with a profound love for each other. Although they obviously enjoyed just being together, their friendship was built on more than sharing recipes and socializing. They had been knit together by years of Bible study and prayer. They were truly sisters in Christ.

During the years we knew them, the love they extended to us made us feel very warm and appreciated in a place where we had no family and many frustrations. They met with us weekly for prayer. They reached out in kindness and acceptance to the neighborhood kids who began coming to the church youth groups. They gave, often sacrificially, to help kids attend camps and retreats. They cooked every Wednesday afternoon to provide a supper for the Youth Club program. They turned out faithfully and enthusiastically for every event the young people participated in or sponsored. They hugged, they laughed, and they cared.

What an example they were to us and to the young people of that community! The love that lit up their lives left no doubts about their genuine faith and discipleship to Christ.

JAMES 5:7–15

Be patient, then, brothers, until the Lord's coming. (James 5:7a)

Knowing the realities and challenges of everyday life can be both frustrating and painful, James writes to encourage his fellow Christians to stand firm in their faith. Not only did those First century believers face what we might recognize as a very familiar sort of belittling of their Christian values and lifestyle choices, but they also often suffered deliberate ostracism, persecution, and even martyrdom because of their faith.

Using a word picture drawn from farming, James assures us that although it may seem a long time until we see the harvest of our inside-the-heart faith and the outside expression of it, that harvest will come. It is God who provides the rain to make the crop grow and He will bring in the ripened grain. In verse 8, James repeats the assurance he gave at the beginning of this section. The Lord is coming again—we can be absolutely certain of that. In the meantime, we are to stand firm and strong on what we know about God and His love for us and be patient toward each other. Complaining and finding fault with our fellow Christians will be detrimental to the health of the Body of Christ and its witness. It's God's standard we have been entrusted to uphold, and He will give us the stamina we need to stand firm.

Beginning in verse 10, James reminds us of an example of faith under fire from the Old Testament. The prophets were God's spokesmen as they pointed out how the people had rejected God's laws and turned their backs on the importance of an inside-the-heart relationship with Him. The prophets warned of the judgment that would come if they did not repent, but also spoke of the future and how God would draw them back to Himself. Because they wrote during such difficult times and their message was very unpopular, many of the prophets suffered ridicule, persecution, and even death. Although standing strong in their faith was not easy, they persevered. Patience in suffering was possible because God stood with them and His compassion and mercy in those trying circumstances brought blessing into their lives. James' encouragement to us is that God will stand with us in the same way if we have put our faith in Him.

Because we know God cares and we can depend on His presence in our lives, we don't need to use phrases like "I swear to God" in our speech to try to impress others. (verse 12) James affirms that because we have that inside-the-heart relationship with God, the outside words we speak should have the reputation of being true. Yes is yes and no is no. What we say should be recognized as the truth and have no need to be embellished with an oath.

Getting Personal...
Why Inside Out Matters

I believe with all my heart that when we allow God into the circumstances of our lives, good or bad, He not only gives us what we need of His strength and peace in that moment, but He also uses those experiences in the future both to grow our own faith and relationship to Him, and to allow us to touch the lives of others. We were created to be all that God can enable us to be, to flourish in the calling He has given us, to be part of an encouraging and enriching Christian community.

We moved to Cedar Falls in August over three decades ago, and for the most part things got off to a pretty smooth start. Our daughter liked 2nd grade and our son loved the parsonage's big yard. I was busy, and for the most part adjusting well, but after years in youth ministry, I still had this nagging angst about whether or not I was doing this senior pastor's wife thing right.

Then God stepped into the routines of my life and did an amazing thing that changed me forever. It was the week of Thanksgiving and I had been fighting a nasty cold which kept getting worse and worse, and I felt awful. The day after Thanksgiving I made an appointment with a doctor and an hour later was admitted to the hospital with pneumonia. I don't believe I have ever been so sick or felt so alone. My husband couldn't stay with me very long because our kids needed him. In that moment of physical pain, fear of the unknown, and the sense of being totally helpless, I cried out in desperation to God. And incredibly, I suddenly felt an almost tangible peace settle over me. There in that very unlikely place, God had definitely gotten my attention.

My husband and I come from small families and have joked that we could hold a family reunion in a closet. But during that week in the hospital I began to experience a new kind of family. My children were lovingly cared for, meals were provided, people came to see me and we were able just to spend time getting to know each other, I was offered the opportunity of teaching an adult SS class when I felt better, and our son's 3rd birthday was celebrated, complete with a John Deere cake.

But the miracle was much more than the kindness shown us in a time of need: It was the beginning of something that has been an integral part of our lives ever since. I discovered that this church was not only part of the Body of Christ, but was also in a very real way the family into which God had called us. The relationships we have had with so many members of the congregation are grounded on the common faith we have in God's unconditional love and His willingness to walk with us in all the circumstances of life, both those that are filled with joy, and those that try us to the limit. The blessing that has infused those relationships has been honest and open and real.

Since that week in the hospital, I have never worried about a role I had to play or fitting into some kind of a pastor's wife mold. What I've discovered is that being part of God's family is like being woven into a beautiful fabric; the intricacies of the design are His creation and the finished product always remains a work in progress. We get to experience the weaving, to feel the thread of our lives intertwined with those around us who share our faith, and to know that what we are together in His hands is more than we could ever be alone. What a blessing to experience being a part of the tapestry that is the Body of Christ!

JAMES 5:16-20

The prayer of a righteous man is powerful and effective. (James 5:16b)

James' closing words in the final section of his epistle contain some very practical and important instructions about how the Body of Christ can thrive, both in good times and when problems arise. If a member of our fellowship is experiencing trouble, we should pray for him. When our hearts are rejoicing over the way God has blessed our lives, we should pour out our praise in music. When a Christian brother or sister is dealing with an illness or another health issue, prayer is the best medicine we can offer. James emphasizes that praying for that person should be something we do as a fellowship of believers.

James is not just talking about the healing of physical ailments, however; he is also referring to the spiritual sickness that can be caused by sin. As Christians our relationships with other Christians should be honest and open, based on the love God has shown us. When that level of Christian community exists, we can help each other in a constructive way deal with sin that has affected another believer's own faith—inside and outside—and may also have impacted the Body of Christ as a whole.

James lists three necessary parts of that kind of spiritual healing: Confession, prayer, and forgiveness. In verse 16, he emphasizes the importance of prayer. Prayer is our intimate conversation with God that is possible because of the inside-the-heart relationship we have with Him. When we are willing to communicate with God and give Him control of the complications of situations we face, we can expect our prayers to be answered. Sometimes the answer God gives far exceeds any resolution we could have imagined. Through the pages of scripture and in the real-life experiences of Christians we know, we can see example after example of how God can bring His kind of good out of the worst of circumstances.

To reinforce how powerful prayer can be, in verses 17 and 18, James reminds us of how God answered the prophet Elijah's prayers during a troubling time in Israel's history. As a man of God, Elijah's concern was that people would realize how pagan idolatry had polluted every area of their lives and see how crucial it was to repent and turn, once again, to obeying God. His prayer was for God to act in a way that would grab their attention—open their eyes—and God answered his prayer in this amazing way. If the prayers of Elijah, who was a man like us, were heard and answered, James writes that we can also have confidence in knowing our prayers will be heard.

In the last two verses of his epistle, James gives one final word of encouragement about how the Body of Christ can remain strong and unified in their faith: We should care so deeply about other Christians that we are willing to reach out to them if they have gotten off track spiritually. Remembering what James has already said about the danger of being judgmental of others, we can know that is not what he is suggesting. Instead, he is describing an act of brotherly love. Because of the inside-the-heart faith we share with other Christians, because we are one in Christ, we must do everything we can to help each other if one of us has "wandered from the truth" and lovingly help to bring that person back. That kind of genuine and honest Christian love can make all the difference in the world as we face the realities of life together.

Getting Personal...
Why Inside Out Matters

Every year the high school students in the church where we were in youth ministry, devoted a lot of time and effort during the winter months practicing and preparing a Christian musical to "take on the road" the next summer. It was a big deal to all of us and the kids poured their energy and enthusiasm into every aspect of the production.

When summer came, besides performing in our own area, we would plan a several-day bus trip, traveling to other locations and churches to present the musical. It wasn't just the performing that had them excited, it was also the opportunity to share their personal faith and what Jesus meant to them.

One summer they decided to include a time in the middle of the performance when they could go into the audience and pray with people who might have a specific request or need. It was a brave and "out of the box" plan for them, and as adults, we hoped it would prove be a good experience for them. One of the first performances they gave was in a church in San Diego, with a plan was to do it again on the beach the next afternoon, hoping to reach some people with the gospel message who didn't usually go to church.

There happened to be a girl at the church that night who was confined to a wheelchair and liked the musical so much that she persuaded her parents to take her to the beach the next day so she could hang our with our youth group and hear the musical again. She came to the beach in her wheelchair with a couple of other kids from her church and spent the afternoon getting to know our group better. When it came time to start performing, she and her friends were an enthusiastic part of the audience along with the curious beach goers that had gathered.

When the time came to invite people in the audience to pray with members of the choir, we saw several of our kids heading straight for the girl in the wheelchair. We suddenly realized that they were probably going to pray that she could walk again, and we had the sinking feeling that they would be very disappointed if that didn't happen. Oh we of little faith! As our kids stood and knelt around her wheelchair, she put her hands on the arm rests and began to push herself up. The kids closest to her reached out to help her, and she cautiously stood up. And then, supported by kids on each side, she began to take tentative steps. Everyone who saw what had just happened was in awe. This girl who had been confined to a wheelchair because of a crippling injury was on her feet and walking!

The rest of the afternoon was a blur for all of us and I'm not even sure if the choir actually finished their performance. But none of us would ever forget the prayers we had seen answered on that beach. Both my husband and I were humbled by our own lack of faith that had caused our doubt when we saw the kids praying, and were totally amazed by how that miracle increased the committed faith of the youth group. When the girl's parents came to pick her up later in the afternoon, they couldn't believe their eyes as she slowly stood up and then took a step toward them.

Although God doesn't always do the miraculous, He has promised that He will always answer our prayers. Why is it so hard for us to trust His steadfast love and faithfulness? Why are we often so slow to turn to Him in prayer? Prayer really does change things; it's our communication with God and the way we invite Him into the circumstances of our lives.

How Do His Words Touch My Life?

What examples can you think of that demonstrate how wealth and the desire to obtain it can go very wrong?

We are all in a time of waiting for the Lord's coming in the future. With that fact in view, how should we live in the present?

James refers to Elijah the prophet as an example of a man who prayed with the confidence that God would answer. Other prophets like Jeremiah, Isaiah, and Daniel also bravely lived out their faith in difficult and dangerous circumstances, relying on the power of prayer to sustain them and help them to stand strong. What are some of the hard things that believers have to face in our world today?

What do we need to pray for when our faith is being tested and challenged?

Sometimes our tendency is to focus on the things we pray about and not on the way God answers. In what circumstances have you been part of or witnessed answered prayer? What impact did that have on your own faith?

In verses 13-16, James writes about several behaviors that need to be in place for a fellowship of Christians to be healthy and grow. How would you describe those essential components that should characterize a church?

Which seem the most natural to put into practice?

Which are more difficult? Why?

A FINAL WORD

Throughout his epistle, James has consistently presented the principle of having an inside-the-heart faith that is demonstrated outside in the way we live. Although we know our faith will be tested by temptations, we can also be confident that God will provide the spiritual stamina it takes to resist and stand firm.

Because we have been born again—transformed on the inside by the salvation we have in Jesus—our faith should be obvious to others by the way we speak and in the things we do. Having genuine faith will motivate us to turn away from ideas and behaviors that might lead us in the wrong direction spiritually. When our faith is tested by difficult situations, or if we experience persecution, God has promised He will give us the strength and patience we need to persevere. Because of our faith and the inside-the-heart relationship we have with God, we can communicate with Him through prayer and have the assurance that God does hear us and will answer.

From the beginning to the end of his letter, James addresses very real circumstances and situations of life that are as critically important to us today as they were in the faith journeys of Jewish Christians in the first century. The counsel and wisdom he shares for meeting those challenges is practical and down to earth because of his own experience on his faith journey as a believer in Jesus. Since he had walked this same road himself, he knew well the twists and turns and hills and valleys that might be encountered along the way. But he also knew that because of his relationship with God through Christ, he never had to travel alone or fear what lay ahead.

Living out his faith in Jesus as the promised Messiah of Israel and sharing that truth with others, was the passion that drove James. Contemporary Jewish religious authorities and Romans who did not accept the message of the gospel he preached, recognized him as a man committed to what he believed and as someone whose life clearly demonstrated the fire of faith that burned within him. Because of how he lived out what he believed, he was commonly referred to by his countrymen as "James the Just". Toward the end of his life, James was also described as "camel knees" because he spent so much time on his knees in prayer. Whether that moniker was used as a way of affirming his lifestyle of faith, or as a term of ridicule—the fact remains the same: James was a man whose inside-the-heart convictions clothed the man he was on the outside in a way that could not be ignored.

When he was martyred for his faith (ca. 60-62 AD), even contemporary secular historians noted that James was a righteous man who had been unjustly accused and put to death, only because he refused to deny what he believed. When his accusers tried to force him to recant his faith, he stood before them in the Temple courtyard and cried out that Jesus was indeed the "Son of God and the Judge of the world". As he was thrown to the ground and was being stoned by the Temple authorities, he knelt and prayed, "Father, forgive them, they know not what they do."

The legacy James has left through his life and his writings has touched the lives of Christians for over 2000 years and continues powerfully to intersect with our own faith journeys today.

HOW THE MESSAGE OF JAMES' EPISTLE IS AFFIRMED IN OTHER SCRIPTURES

The Bible is an amazing book, written by about 40 human authors over a time span of 1500 years, includes many different types of literature, and was originally written in 3 languages very different from English—and yet its message has a continuity that flows from the first chapters of Genesis to the end of Revelation. Although in one sense it is a "library" of 66 separate books, it is really one whole that stands as God's inspired Word and reveals how a relationship with Him can change our lives.

With this is mind, it is not surprising that what James wrote in his letter echoes the same concepts and themes that appear throughout the Old Testament and are an important part of the teaching ministry of Jesus. The practical issues of faith and life James addresses are also mirrored in the books written by the other leaders of the early church because they were sharing the same message. It is very clear that the inside-the-heart relationship each of them described is only possible because of the price Jesus paid for our sin, and when we have been born again, that should make a real difference in our words and actions that are obvious to others on the outside.

Because all of scripture is, in essence, communicating the same God-given message, looking at what we find in other parts of the Bible that deal with the same topic often gives us a deeper understanding of a text. The following pages provide some examples of other passages of scripture that bear such a connection to James' epistle.

Some of the teachings of Jesus that are reflected in James' letter:

James 1:2	Matt. 5:10-12	James 1:4	Matt. 5:48
James 1:5	Matt. 7:7	James 1:17	Matt. 7:11
James 1:20	Matt. 5:22	James 1:22	Matt. 7:24-27
James 2:5	Matt. 5:3	James 2:8	Mark 12:31
James 2:10	Matt. 5:19	James 2:13	Matt. 5:7
James 2:14	Matt. 7:21	James 3:12	Matt. 7:17
James 3:13	Matt. 5:5	James 4:4	Matt. 6:24
James 4:8	Matt. 5:8	James 4:9	Luke 6:25
James 4:10	Matt. 23:12	James 4:11	Matt. 5:22
James 5:1	Matt. 19:23	James 5:2	Matt. 6:20
James 5:12	Matt. 5:34-35	James 5:19-20	Matt. 18:5

We are made new on the inside because of the salvation God provides:

Jer. 31:31-33	Ezek. 36:25-27	Isaiah 61:10
John 3:16	John 15:6	2 Cor. 5:17-21
Titus 3:4-7	2 Cor. 3:18	Phil. 3:7-9
Rom. 3:20-24	Gal. 2:20	1 John 1:8-9
Eph. 4:22-24	Eph. 2:8-9	

Our inside-the-heart faith should be evident in what we do:

Prov. 10:21-30	Prov. 3:1-6	Ps. 1:1-3
Gal. 6:7-10	1 Cor. 9:24-27	Gal. 5:19-26
1 John 5:1-5	1 John 2:3-6	2 Peter 1:5-8

About persevering in our faith:

Phil. 4:12-13	1 Peter 2:19-23	1 Peter 4:12-13
1 Peter 1:3-7	1 Cor. 9:24-27	Heb. 12:1-3
John 16:33		

The importance of resisting temptations:

Rom. 6:1-14	1 Cor. 10:11-13	2 Cor. 7:1
Eph. 6:10-13	Heb. 2:18	1 John 5:2-5
1 Peter 5:8-9		

Why our words matter:

Prov. 10:19-20	Prov. 15:1, 4	Prov. 12:18
Prov. 25:11-12	Prov. 21:23	Ps. 19:14
Luke 6:45	Matt. 12:35-37	Eph. 4:29
Col. 4:6		

Why we can be sure God "walks" with us on our faith journey:

Jer. 29:11-13	Prov. 2:6	Prov. 3:5-6
Ex. 33:13-14	Ps. 119:105	Ps. 37:23-24
Eph. 1:4-6	Phil. 1:6	Phil. 2:12-13

What should characterize our worship and relationships with other believers:

Ps. 92:1	Ps. 47:1-2	Ps. 100
Matt. 18:19-20	1 Thes. 5:12-22	Eph. 4:11-16
1 John 1:5-7	1 John 4:7-8	Col. 3:12-17
Col. 4:2	Eph. 5:15-21	Gal. 3:26-29
Rom. 14:10, 12-13	Eph. 4:32	2 Cor. 1:3-5

Having the right perspective on material possessions:

Prov. 11:28	Prov. 15:6	Prov. 22:1-2, 16
Prov. 28:22	Matt. 6:31-32	Phil. 4:19
2 Cor. 9:6-12	1 Tim. 6:6-10	Rom. 12:16
1 John 2:15-17	Heb. 13:5	

True wisdom comes from God:

Prov. 2:3-5	Prov. 2:6-7	Prov. 9:10
Is. 2:3	John 8:12	Col. 3:16-20
Eph. 5:15-16	1 Cor. 1:20-25	1 Cor. 3:18-20

God hears and answers our prayers:

Ps. 65:2-4	Ps. 91:14-16	Ps. 138:1-3
Jer. 29:12-13	Rom. 8:26-27	Phil. 4:6-7
1 John 5:14-15		

How we should live as we anticipate the Lord's return:

2 Peter 3:10-18	Heb. 10:24-2
1 Peter 4:7-11	1 Thes. 5:12-22

ABOUT SALLY BAKER

Sally Baker was reared in Rockford, Illinois where she did her undergraduate and graduate work at Rockford College. Sally and her husband Ed have been involved in ministry in Denver CO; Des Moines, IA, and for the past 33 years, in Cedar Falls, IA, where Sally has written and taught many Bible courses for adults and children. She has taught her Square One Bible survey course in several churches and settings. Sally is a pastor's wife, a mother, a grandmother, a mentor to younger women, a leader in her church's children's programming, and a strong voice for the authority, reliability, and applicability of God's Word to all areas of life.